curious about
PEGASUS

BY GINA KAMMER

AMICUS LEARNING

What are you

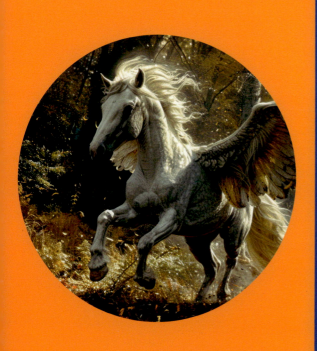

CHAPTER ONE

Pegasus Legends
PAGE
4

2
CHAPTER TWO

Pegasus Life
PAGE
10

curious about?

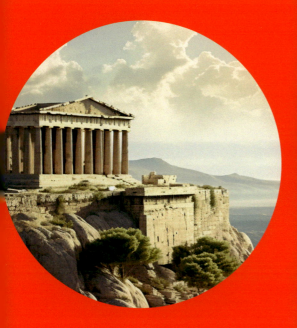

CHAPTER THREE

Finding Pegasus
PAGE
16

Stay Curious! Learn More . . . 22
Glossary 24
Index 24

Curious About is published by
Amicus Learning, an imprint of Amicus
P.O. Box 227
Mankato, MN 56002
www.amicuspublishing.us

Copyright © 2025 Amicus.
International copyright reserved in all countries.
No part of this book may be reproduced in any
form without written permission from the publisher.

Editor: Ana Brauer
Series Designer: Kathleen Petelinsek
Book Designer and Photo Researcher: Kim Pfeffer

Library of Congress Cataloging-in-Publication Data
Names: Kammer, Gina, author.
Title: Curious about Pegasus / by Gina Kammer.
Description: Mankato, MN : Amicus Learning, an imprint of
Amicus, [2025] | Series: Curious about mythical creatures |
Includes bibliographical references and index. | Audience: Ages
6–9 | Audience: Grades 2–3 | Summary: "What does Pegasus
look like? Learn the Greek mythology surrounding the winged horse
in this question-and-answer book for elementary readers. Includes
infographics, table of contents, glossary, books and websites for
further research, and index"— Provided by publisher.
Identifiers: LCCN 2024017581 (print) | LCCN 2024017582
(ebook) | ISBN 9798892000994 (library binding) | ISBN
9798892001571 (paperback) | ISBN 9798892002158 (ebook)
Subjects: LCSH: Pegasus (Greek mythology)—Miscellanea—
Juvenile literature. Classification: LCC BL820.P4 K36 2025 (print)|
LCC BL820.P4 (ebook) | DDC 398.20938/0454—dc23/
eng20240510
LC record available at https://lccn.loc.gov/2024017581
LC ebook record available at https://lccn.loc.gov/2024017582

Photo Credits: Adobe Stock/comicsans, cover, pengedarseni, 6–7,
SULAIMAN, 11 (top); Yusif, 14; Alamy Stock Photo/Leah Bignell/
Design Pics, 20; British Library/Public Domain, 9 (second from
bottom); Dreamstime/Stockeeco, 9 (top); Freepik/artefacti, 12–13,
fakedav, 11 (bottom), Freepik, 16–17, natttalya, 5, user7351474,
15; Public Domain/9 (bottom); Wikimedia Commons/ Government
of Kazakhstan, 9 (middle), Mary Hamilton Frye, 4, Phuong Huy, 9
(second from top), Public Domain, 21, Theodoor van Thulden, 19

Printed in China

CHAPTER ONE 1

What is a pegasus?

One Greek hero was able to tame and ride Pegasus.

Pegasus is the name of a horse with wings in Greek **myths**. His mother is a monster named Medusa. His father is Poseidon, the god of the sea and horses. Today, any mythical horse with wings is called a pegasus. Some of these horses also have horns.

Pegasus is a symbol of inspiration and creativity.

PEGASUS LEGENDS

Is Pegasus real?

PEGASUS LEGENDS

The Pegasi are a **species** of winged horses. They are the offspring of Pegasus and horses.

Likely not. Yet people long ago and today show horses with wings in art. Pegasus is in many **legends**. Horses with wings seem powerful and beautiful. Pegasi are listed in old books with real animals. But no one has **proof** that they're real.

When did Pegasus legends start?

About 3,000 years ago! In one legend, Poseidon gives Pegasus to a Greek hero named Bellerophon. Together they ride into battle. They fight a monster with three heads. It can breathe fire. But with the help of Pegasus, the hero wins. He flies away on Pegasus. There are also many myths about other winged horses.

GREECE: PEGASUS

CHINA, VIETNAM: LONGMA

KAZAKHSTAN, MONGOLIA: TULPAR

INDONESIA, MALAYSIA: KUDA SEMBERANI

INDIA: UCHCHAIHSHRAVAS

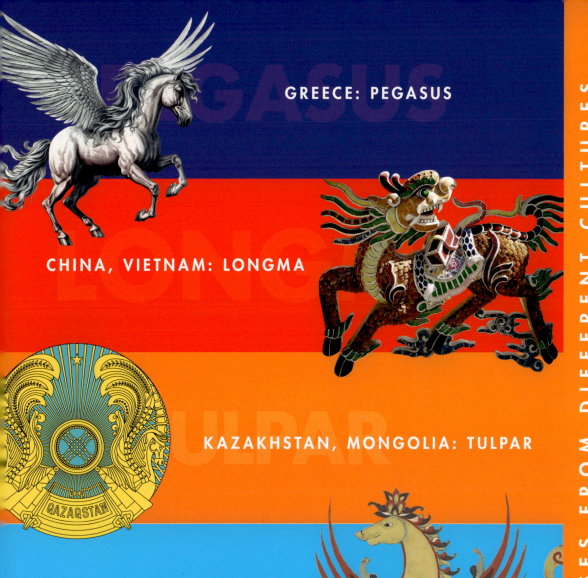

WINGED HORSES FROM DIFFERENT CULTURES

9

CHAPTER TWO

How long does Pegasus live?

Maybe forever! Pegasus is part god. Most stories say he can live forever. But some say he didn't. Instead, he was turned into a group of stars. You can see Pegasus in the sky today. So maybe he still lives on either way.

Pegasus is believed to be **immortal**, like the gods.

PEGASUS STAR CHART

The Pegasus constellation only makes up the front part of the horse. Still, it is one of the largest!

PEGASUS LIFE

What does Pegasus like to do?

PEGASUS LIFE

The name Pegasus means "spring" or "well."

12

Fly! The winged horse loves the sky. In Greek myths, Pegasus can fly as far as Mount Olympus. Olympus is the home of the gods. It is in the heavens. Pegasus also enjoys water. Flying fast makes him thirsty. He likes to drink from pools of water.

PEGASUS LIFE

What magic powers does Pegasus have?

PEGASUS LIFE

Pegasus can fly high into the heavens. He can even carry lightning for Zeus.

A few kinds! Pegasus can carry thunder and lightning for Zeus. Zeus is the king of the Greek gods. With his hoof, Pegasus can make springs! In one story, the Greek muses were singing. A mountain rose too high to listen. Pegasus kicked it. It didn't get too big. Instead, a spring gushed out.

PEGASUS ABILITIES

wings — FLIGHT
head — NEVER TIRED
chest — STRONG
hoof — MAKING SPRINGS
legs — SPEED

CHAPTER THREE

3

FINDING PEGASUS

Where does Pegasus live?

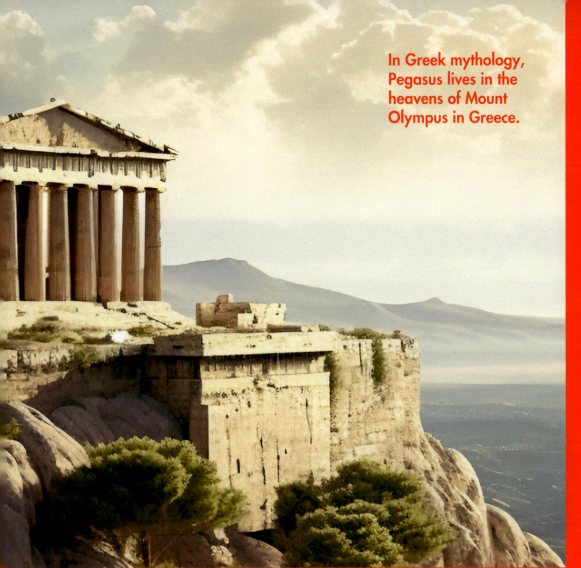

In Greek mythology, Pegasus lives in the heavens of Mount Olympus in Greece.

FINDING PEGASUS

Pegasus lives on Mount Olympus with the gods. He lives like royalty in Zeus's palace! But other Pegasi travel all over the world. Pegasus even travels the stars! Legends also say Pegasi are from the country of Ethiopia. Other winged horses live in different areas.

Is Pegasus friendly?

If you can tame him! But it won't be easy. In one myth, Bellerophon couldn't catch Pegasus. Finally, the goddess of wisdom, Athena, came in a dream. She left him a golden **bridle**. He waited until Pegasus drank from a spring. Then he caught Pegasus. They flew to many adventures!

The Greek goddess, Athena, gave Bellerophon her golden bridle. This helped him catch Pegasus.

FINDING PEGASUS

19

In some stories, a Greek hero named Perseus flew on Pegasus to save a young woman.

Can I fly on Pegasus?

Sure! If you can find him. But maybe you shouldn't. After many adventures with Pegasus, Bellerophon wanted more. He tried to use Pegasus to fly to the gods. Zeus was angry. Pegasus threw the hero from his back. Then, Pegasus got to live on Olympus. He was the greatest of horses.

With the help of Pegasus, Bellerophon killed the Chimera, a fire-breathing creature with three heads.

STAY CURIOUS!

ASK MORE QUESTIONS

What stories have people told about Pegasus?

What can I find out from old Pegasus pictures?

Try a BIG QUESTION: Why do people love to make art and tell stories about Pegasus?

SEARCH FOR ANSWERS

Search the library catalog or the Internet.
A librarian, teacher, or parent can help you.

Using Keywords
Find the looking glass.

Keywords are the most important words in your question.

If you want to know about:
- Pegasus stories, type: PEGASUS MYTHS
- Pegasus in pictures, type: ANCIENT PEGASUS ART

LEARN MORE

FIND GOOD SOURCES

Are the sources reliable?
Some sources are better than others. An adult can help you. Here are some good, safe sources.

Books
Pegasus
by Christine Ha, 2022.

Story of Medusa
by Anna Collins, 2023.

Internet Sites

Britannica Kids: Pegasus
https://kids.britannica.com/kids/article/Pegasus/353609
Britannica is an encyclopedia with educational information on many topics.

Ducksters: Ancient Greece: Monsters and Creatures of Greek Mythology
https://www.ducksters.com/history/ancient_greece/monsters_and_creatures_of_greek_mythology.php
Ducksters has educational articles about many topics for kids.

Every effort has been made to ensure that these websites are appropriate for children. However, because of the nature of the Internet, it is impossible to guarantee that these sites will remain active indefinitely or that their contents will not be altered.

SHARE AND TAKE ACTION

Which stories have winged horses in them today?
Ask an adult to help you search for new stories about Pegasi at the library. Read them together!

Go stargazing.
With the help of an adult, find a clear night to spot constellations from Greek mythology.

What lives in Ethiopia?
Study the birthplace of Pegasi!

GLOSSARY

bridle Leather straps that are put around a horse's head to steer it.

immortal Living forever or never dying.

legend A story from the past that may or may not be true but cannot be checked.

myth An idea or story that is believed by many people but that is not true.

proof Facts or evidence that show something is true.

species A group of living things with similar features that are grouped under a common name and can produce offspring.

INDEX

Athena, 18, 19
Bellerophon, 4, 8, 18, 20–21
constellation, 10–11
flying, 13, 20
Medusa, 4
Mount Olympus, 13, 17
Perseus, 20
Poseidon, 4, 8
powers, 7, 14–15
springs, 12, 15, 18
Zeus, 14, 15, 17, 20

About the Author

Gina Kammer grew up writing and illustrating her own stories. Now she teaches others to write stories at inkybookwyrm.com. She likes reading fantasy and medieval literature. She also enjoys traveling, oil painting, archery, and snuggling her grumpy bunny. She lives in Minnesota.